COLOURS OF THE WILD
Animals of the Americas

Heather Thomas & Russell Thomas

American Alligator

American Alligator (Genus: Alligator)

Length

11.2-15.7 feet (3.4-4.8 m)

Weight

1,230 lbs (560 kg)

Qualities

Strong, dominant

An alligator's size depends on the type and amount of food available. They will prey on anything smaller than themselves, both in the water or near the shore, including fish, birds, snakes, and small **mammals.** Alligators have 75 teeth. Any lost or broken teeth are replaced, and an alligator can grow up to 3,000 new teeth in its lifetime.

How many teeth do you have?

Bighorn Sheep

Bighorn Sheep (Genus: Ovis)

Height

42 inches (100 cm)

Length

63-73 inches (160-185 cm)

Weight

128-315 lbs (58-143 kg)

Qualities

Agile, **Adaptive**

Bighorn sheep live along the length of the Rocky Mountains. They have an amazing sense of balance and can run up and down cliffs and mountains without falling.

Can you imagine standing on ledges only 2 inches (5 cm) wide and jumping across gaps of up to 20 feet (6 m)?

Bb

Caribou

Caribou (Genus: Rangifer)

Height	Length	Weight	Qualities
39-47 inches (100-120 cm) to the shoulder	70-82 inches (180-210 cm)	220-462 lbs (100-210 kg)	Resourceful, Independent

Both male and female woodland caribou have unique flat, dense antlers that begin as velvet-covered bumps every spring. These grow up to 1 inch (2.5 cm) every day until late summer, when they are over 3 feet (1 m) in length. Caribou are **solitary, elusive** animals that are rarely seen.

Do you think you could live in the forest like a caribou, eating **lichen** and small plants?

Downy Woodpecker

Downy Woodpecker (Genus: Dryobates)

Height	Weight	Qualities
5.5-7.0 inches (14-18 cm)	0.7-1.16 oz (20-32 g)	Small, Powerful

The adult downy woodpecker has a strong beak and can repeatedly drum into a tree up to 20 times per second, for a total of 10,000 to 12,000 pecks per day.

Do you think you would get a headache from pecking so much?

Dd

Eagle

Eagle (Genus: Haliaeetus)

Height

27.9-37.8 inches (71-96 cm)

Weight

6.6-13.8 lbs (3-6.3 kg)

Qualities

Bold, Instinctive

The bald eagle is one of the largest birds of prey, with a strong beak and talons. It has a wingspan of 80 inches (2 m). An eagle can fly as high as 15,000 feet (4,572 m) and as fast as 99 miles/hr (160 km/hr).

What do you think it would be like to spread your arms and fly as high and fast as an eagle?

fox

Fox (Genus: Vulpes)

Height

14-20 inches (35-50 cm) to the shoulder

Length

18-35 inches (45-90 cm) (excluding tail)

Weight

6.6-35 lbs (3-14 kg)

Qualities

Clever, Fast

The red fox is the largest and most common of the North American foxes. Foxes have been known to leap over a 6-foot fence (2 m) and can run at a speed of 30 miles/hr (48 km/hr). They can hear mice squeak from 100 feet (33 m) away and detect sounds underground or snow at over 25 feet (7.6 m).

Do you think you could hear a mouse moving around underground?

Grizzly Bear

Grizzly Bear (Genus: Ursus)

Height	Length	Weight	Qualities
3.35 feet (102 cm) to the shoulder	6.5 feet (198 cm)	1000lbs (about 500kg)	Hungry, Protective

The hump between their shoulders is one of the differences between grizzlies and other bears. It is a large muscle that helps them dig and catch prey. Larger grizzlies can lift more than 1,000 lbs (500 kg). Grizzlies can run up to 30 miles/hr (48 km/h), climb trees, and swim. They are **omnivores** and eat up to 90 lbs (40 kg) of insects, fruit, plants, and meat every day. Grizzly bears need a lot of food to survive the winter and can gain over 2 lbs (0.9 kg) per day.

What should you do if you see a grizzly bear?

Harbour Seal

Harbour Seal (Genus: Phoca)

Length	Weight	Qualities
6.1 feet (185 cm)	120-370 lbs (55–168 kg)	Playful, Determined

While harbour seals are commonly found all over the world. These **mammals** are curious creatures and sometimes swim and play with divers. They will swim up to 31 miles (50 km) from their home resting place and dive up to 300 feet (91 m) to find food. They eat a variety of fish, squid, molluscs, and **crustaceans.**

Do you like seafood? Have you ever eaten it raw?

Ibis

Ibis (Genus: Plegadis)

Length

18-22 inches (46-56 cm)

Weight

16-18.5 oz (450-525 g)

Qualities

Alert, Focused

The white-faced ibis is a bird with dark, glossy **plumage** that is multi-coloured in the sun. They are **migrating** birds that live in marshes and **wetlands** from as far north as Canada to as far south as Chile and Argentina. The North American birds stay within Canada and the United States, while the South American birds remain in Brazil, Chile, and Argentina.

Would you rather stay in one place all year or travel when the seasons change?

Jackrabbit

Jackrabbit (Genus: Lepus)

Height

18-22 inches (46-56 cm)

Weight

16-18.5 oz (450-525 g)

Qualities

Cautious, Swift

Jackrabbits are careful, cautious creatures. They are skittish and live **solitary** lives and shed their fur, changing colour to better **camouflage** themselves based on the season. Jackrabbits are fast runners and can avoid predators by hopping up to 50 miles/hr (80 km/hr) for short bursts.

How fast can you run?

Killer Whale or Orca

Killer Whale or Orca (Genus: Orcinus)

Length

Female: 16-23 feet (5-7 m),
Male: 20-26 feet (6-8 m)

Weight

4-6 tonnes

Qualities

Intelligent, Social

Orcas are the largest member of the dolphin family and can be found in almost every ocean, even the Arctic. They have enormous brains, weighing up to 15 lbs (6.8 kg), which they use for hunting and socializing. A family of orcas is called a pod. Each pod is led by a **matriarch** and uses slightly different tactics for communicating and hunting.

What other animal **species** have a **matriarch** as a leader?

Loon

Loon (Genus: Gavia)

Length

26-36 inches (66-91 cm)

Weight

5-16.8 lbs (2.2-7.6 kg)

Qualities

Nurturing, Dedicated

Common loons are freshwater birds that can hold their breath for 90 seconds and dive up to 33 feet (10 m) to catch fish. They can live up to 30 years and may have several mates during that time. Both parents take care of sitting on the eggs. After hatching, their chicks are fed every hour for 3 months. Loons allow their babies to sit on their backs when the little ones get tired of swimming.

Have you ever ridden on your parent's back?

Muskox

Muskox (Genus: Ovibos)

Height	Length	Weight	Qualities
4-5 feet (1.1-1.5 m)	Female: 4.4-6.6 feet (135-200 cm), Male: 6.6-8.2 feet (200-250 cm)	400-900 lbs (180-410 kg)	Hardy, Protective

The muskox has a coat of thick, heavy hair that keeps them warm in the cold Arctic air. The hair is a mix of stiff guard hairs on the surface and thick, wool-like fur underneath. This special undercoat is shed every summer when the temperature rises. Muskox hair is warmer than sheep's wool and softer than cashmere, which makes it very expensive wool at $40-80 per ounce (28 g).

They are named for the strong scent that males use to attract females during the breeding season. What face do you think you would make if you smelled a muskox?

Mm

Narwhal

Narwhal (Genus: Monodon)

Length	Weight	Qualities
17 feet (5.18 m) (excluding tusk)	up to 4,200 lbs (1,905 kg)	Sensitive, Social

Male narwhals, also known as the "unicorns of the sea," can grow tusks up to 10 feet (3 m) long. The tusk is an inside-out tooth with over 10 million nerve endings, making it sensitive to changes in ocean water. A narwhal's tusk can bend up to 12 inches or 30 cm before breaking, and it is used to create holes in the ice for breathing and to find food and other narwals in the ocean.

Not all narwhals have tusks. What else do you think they use to help find their food?

Nn

Owl

Owl (Genus: Bubo)

Length

17-25 inches (43-64 cm)

Weight

2.6-3.5 lbs (1.2kg-1.6 kg); males are smaller than females

Qualities

Adaptable, Accurate

The great horned owl can be recognized by its size and the ear tufts that stick out above its head like horns. As fierce hunters, they hunt small to medium-sized animals and birds at night. Their talons are so strong that they have as much gripping power as a golden eagle. Owls will eat their prey whole or tear it into pieces. After **digestion,** they throw up pellets filled with bones and other **inedible** bits.

Have you ever found an owl's favourite tree by looking for pellets on the ground below?

Puffin

Puffin (Genus: Fraterculini)

Length	Weight	Qualities
10 inches (25 cm)	17.5 oz (500 g)	Water-loving, Agile

Atlantic puffins are sometimes called "clowns of the sea" and "sea parrots" because of their black and white **plumage** and parrot-like beak. These small birds fly quickly, up to 55 miles/hr (88 km/hr), as they beat their wings 400 times per minute. Puffins can dive as deep as 197 feet (60 m) into the ocean. A puffin's mouth has a spiny **upper palate** and a raspy tongue, which helps it catch and hold up to 12 small fish in its beak at once.

Puffins prefer to spend their time on the water. What do you think it would be like to live on the water for most of your life?

Pp

Quail

Quail (Genus: Callipepla)

Length

9.4-10.6 inches (24-27 cm)

Weight

4.9-8.1 oz (140-230 g)

Qualities

Social, Resilient

Quail are **tolerant** of people and **adaptable** to new environments. This means that groups of them are often found together in parks or under bushes in **urban** areas, as well as in the wild along the length of the west coast from California up to Canada. Quail do not need to drink water to survive. Instead, they eat plants and insects with higher water content.

What kinds of insects do you think quail find juicy and delicious?

Raven

Raven (Genus: Corvus)

Length

21-26 inches (54-67 cm)

Weight

1.5-4.4 lbs (0.7-2.2 kg)

Qualities

Observant, Problem-Solver

The common raven is a hardy bird that is found in many climates. Ravens are intelligent and can pre-plan tasks, use tools, and work together in groups to hunt other birds or small animals. They are extremely vocal and communicate in gurgles, clucks, chuckles, and caws. Sometimes they will even imitate sounds around them, including human conversation.

What kinds of sounds would you make if you were talking with a raven?

Squirrel

Squirrel (Genus: Tamiasciurus)

Length

10-15 inches (25-38 cm) (including tail)

Weight

7-8.8 oz (200-250 g)

Qualities

Determined, Quick

American red squirrels are found in forested areas across Canada and the United States. These **rodents** are bold when it comes to tracking down food. In the wild, they eat seeds, pinecones, plants, fungi, and nuts, but in **urban** areas, they will leap onto bird feeders, eat food left on picnic tables, and sometimes even gnaw their way into cabins. Squirrels use their tail to help them balance when running, leaping, and climbing trees. They are great at figuring out puzzles and completing obstacle courses to get food and treats.

Do you like running through obstacle courses?

Ss

Turtle

Turtle (Genus: Terrapene)

Length	Weight	Qualities
4-8 inches (10-20 cm)	2 lbs (907 g)	Independent, Slow

American box turtles are named for their ability to pull in their legs and heads and form the shape of a box with their shell. Their diet consists of plants, mushrooms, berries, worms, caterpillars, slugs, and bird eggs. They live alone in wooded areas, grasslands, and near ponds or streams, never ranging more than 250 yards (229 m) from their home base.

Can you imagine living your whole life, like a box turtle, in a space the size of a tennis court?

Utah Prairie Dog

Utah Prairie Dog (Genus: Cynomys)

Length

12-14 inches (30-36 cm), as well as a 1-2.3 inch long (3-6 cm) tail

Weight

1.7-3 lbs (0.77-1.41 kg)

Qualities

Organized, Focused

The Utah prairie dog is a **rodent** that eats grasses, seeds, flowers, and sometimes insects. An underground prairie dog **burrow** is usually the size of an acre and is called a "town," with separate areas for sleeping, eating, having babies, and passing waste. It may have up to 70 entrances for one family, or **coterie**, of prairie dogs. These families are divided into sub-groups known as "wards" within the "town."

Do you think you could live with all your grandparents, uncles and aunts, sisters, brothers, and cousins at the same time?

Uu

Vulture

Vulture (Genus: Sarcoramphus)

Length

26-32 inches (67-81 cm)

Weight

6-10 lbs (2.7-4.5 kg)

Qualities

Sensitive to Smell

With a wingspan of up to 7 feet (2 m), the king vulture is the largest vulture in Central and South America and can soar high in the sky for hours. As **scavengers,** vultures are an important part of the food chain. They have developed featherless heads and necks to keep themselves clean from the dead animals they eat.

A vulture's food would be incredibly smelly to humans. What's the worst thing you've ever smelled?

Wolf

Wolf (Genus: Canis)

Height

27-36 inches (68-91 cm) at the shoulder

Weight

93-112 lbs (42-51 kg)

Qualities

Social, Good Hunters

Northwestern or timber wolves can hear 20 times better than humans, and their sense of smell is 100 times stronger. At the top of the food chain, wolves are impressive hunters that work together as a pack to take down much larger animals. They help keep **ecosystems** healthy by keeping deer and elk **populations** from getting too large. There are usually 5-11 wolves in a pack, but sometimes groups of 20 or 30 can be found living together.

Wolves sometimes howl to communicate. Can you howl like a wolf?

Xenarthran

Xenarthran means unusual joints. Sloths are part of this superorder because their joints and claws are designed for climbing and hanging upside down from trees.

Three-Toed Sloth (Genus: Bradypus)

Height	Weight	Qualities
18 inches (0.45 m)	8-10 lbs (3.6-4.5 kg)	Quiet, Slow

Sloths are **vegetarians** and eat leaves, buds, and shoots, but because they have a slow digestive system, it takes up to 30 days to **metabolize** their food. The kings and queens of slow motion, sloths move only 1 foot (30 cm) per minute on land. In water, they can swim up to 3 times faster and can hold their breath for up to 40 minutes.

Do you move faster on land or in water?

Yellow-Headed Blackbird

Yellow-Headed Blackbird (Genus: Xanthocephalus)

Height

8-10 inches (21-26 cm)

Weight

1.6-3.5 oz (44-100 g)

Qualities

Territorial, Domineering

The yellow-headed blackbird is about the size of a robin with a big head and dominates the smaller red-winged blackbird for preferred nesting sites among the reeds of prairie **wetlands.** Yellow-headed blackbirds forage as a flock for food in a field, playing leapfrog with each other. This makes it look like the whole flock is rolling across the top of a field like black water.

Have you played leapfrog? How many times can you jump over your friend's back?

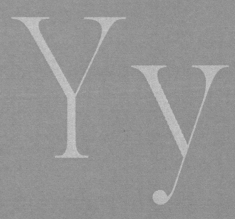

Yy

Zebu

Zebu (Genus: Bos)

Length

5.25 feet (1600 cm)

Weight

1,000 lbs (454 kg)

Qualities

Resilient, Hardy

Zebu or Ongole cattle are named for a tall hump that sits above their shoulders and is larger in males than females. The Zebu is highly **resistant to disease** and has a slower **metabolism,** making them easy to raise on rough land. They are drought **tolerant** with more efficient sweat glands than other cattle, making them ideal for the tropical and sub-tropical climates of Brazil.

South American Zebus were imported from India. What do you think the first zebus did when they stepped off the boat that brought them to Brazil?

Zz

GLOSSARY

Adaptable	Able to change habits or gain skills required to suit the environment
Burrow	A hole or tunnel dug by a small animal that is used for living in
Camouflage	To hide or disguise itself by changing the way it looks
Coterie	A large family of prairie dogs
Crustacean	A legged sea animal with a shell (lobster, crab, or shrimp)
Digestion	To break down and absorb food inside your body
Elusive	Difficult to find or catch
Ecosystem	The interconnection of plants and animals in the environment
Habitat	A place where the conditions are right for an animal to live
Inedible	Not able to eat or digest
Lichen	A plant-like organism that grows with algae and fungus together, often hard and bumpy
Mammal	Warm-blooded animal with hair that provides milk for its young
Matriarch	Female leader of a family
Metabolism	Rate of digestion in an animal's body
Migrating	Moving from place to place according to the season
Organism	A complete living thing

Omnivore	An animal that eats both plants and meat
Plumage	Feathers on a bird
Populations	A collection of animals or people in a specific area
Resistant to disease	Immune to disease, doesn't get sick easily
Rodent	A mammal with large front teeth whose growth is worn down by gnawing
Scavenger	An animal that eats leftover or rotting food
Solitary	Being alone or by oneself
Species	A group of animals that have the same characteristics (i.e., bears)
Territorial	A behaviour where animals will protect their habitat
Tolerant	Ability to live in less-than-ideal conditions or can handle a variety of environments
Upper palate	Roof of the mouth
Urban	Cities or towns
Vegetarian	Eating plants, fruits, nuts, and seeds. Not eating meat
Wetland	Soggy marshland in or near water where many different species live
Xenarthran	The superorder of animal species with unusual joints designed for hanging

Find Out More

All About Birds - Bird Facts: https://www.allaboutbirds.org/

Just Fun Facts – Fun Animal Facts: https://justfunfacts.com/

Kidadl - Fun Animal Facts: https://kidadl.com/

One Kind Planet - Fun Animal Facts: https://onekindplanet.org/

Tree Hugger – Animal Facts: https://www.treehugger.com/